A quick word to grown-ups reading this.

Bebo the Hero
is a story for young children about a cat who lives in a home with lots of other cats.

The peace is spoilt when one cat starts to bully the others, and even the dog.

We follow Bebo as he sets out to restore harmony.

We hope this book will help children to talk about the difficult topic of bullying.

This is a very special house. A house where cats can come and live when they don't have a home of their own. This is a story that happened many meows ago.

Tizzy was sitting by the fire. All the cats love this spot, because it is warm and comfy. Along with eating and making holes in the curtains, lying next to the fire is the best cat thing to do.

Tizzy was very worried because …

... THERE WAS A NEW KITTEN IN THE HOUSE!
The kitten's name was Ted.

Ted wanted to be in all the same comfy seats and corners as Tizzy, because they are the best places to be. Tizzy was not at all happy about this. Being so much bigger than the tiny kitten, Tizzy started pushing Ted around and being mean. The big cat hoped that being nasty would make the new arrival go away.

Ted is very small and easy to bully. If you are bigger and stronger, or if you know a place better than someone else, you must be careful not to scare those ...

who are new, or feeling small.

Kitten Ted didn't stay small for long.

Ted grew and grew and grew! Ted had learned a very bad lesson about bullying and now started being mean to Tizzy.

Ted would choose high places, like the giant garden flowerpot, and leap onto poor Tizzy.

Ted had become very naughty; bossing everyone around. Ted was controlling the other cats and telling them all what to do.

Ted was particularly mean to a beautiful black cat called Scatch. One day Ted jumped on Scatch so roughly that Scatch had to go to the vet with a bad leg.

Poor Scatch ended up in the cat hospital. The vet was wonderful and did what they could. Even so, every one of Scatch's steps now made a knocking noise because of the plaster cast.

Its very hard to be a cat when you can't even walk properly.

Ted did more and more terrible things; pushing the wobbly Scatch over, upsetting Tizzy and even annoying Tess the dog. Dogs aren't usually bothered about the endless meowing nonsense of cats, but this was getting silly.

Scatch couldn't even run away.

When Ted started eating not only food from his own bowl but Scatch's too, Scatch decided to leave home. The special house didn't seem special anymore.

Feeling very sad, poor Scatch headed out into the big wide world.

Now this is a strange story, because so far it has not involved Bebo.

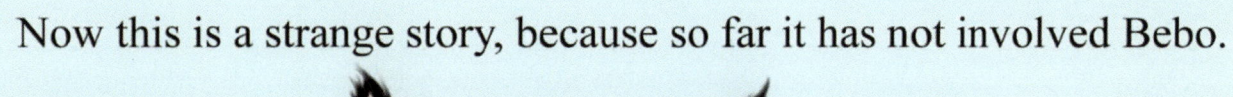

A big, old, fluffy, grumpy black and white cat.

Bebo is the cat this story is all about.

Bebo had seen it all before. He usually kept out of the way of all the silly cats and their fighting.

When the house started not being safe, Bebo went into action. He went straight to Ted and gave him a good meowing at!

Bebo was going to set out to find Scatch. Bebo the hero. He was the one who wanted to stop all the bullying and was brave enough to help his friend.

If Bebo was going to be a superhero ...

he was going to need

A CAPE!!

Scatch was scared and alone in the local park, scared and hungry. With his injured leg he couldn't even catch mice. It was getting dark and there were foxes around. Life seemed very hard for a lopsided cat in a plaster cast.

Bebo ran around the park searching for Scatch. Over the hills, through the long grass, by the pond and behind trees, Bebo looked everywhere. Even though he was old, Bebo kept going. Nothing could stop the superhero.

Bebo made sure Scatch was comfortable,

and feeling safe,

but Bebo was still cross. He wanted to make sure it never happened again.

Bebo gathered all the other cats around. They did what they were told. Our fluffy superhero was far too big and old to argue with. Red cape or not, they were all going to have to listen. Telling someone older, like Bebo, is very sensible if you are being bullied. Sometimes you need someone bigger and more grown-up, like Bebo, to help sort things out.

In the end, Ted and Tizzy realised that what they had done was wrong. Scatch forgave Ted, once he'd had a good meow about it, and they even learned to share the spot by the fire. It's very easy when you are being bullied to think that bullying is normal.

Poor little Ted had turned into angry mean Ted but, now they were all friends again, everything was just ...

purr-fect.

Bebo made it very clear that anyone being a bully would have to answer to him.

As the story ends, Tess probably wondered if it would be easier to live with dogs. All that meowing and drama was a bit much. As for Bebo ...

...he hung up his cape and went to bed.

THE END

Printed in Great Britain
by Amazon